Owls

Elizabeth Russell-Arnot

Contents

Owls are nocturnal

Most owls are **nocturnal** birds.
This means that they sleep in the daytime
and are awake at night.

Most owls go hunting
for their food at night.

Owl sounds

Different owls make different sounds.

Barn owls make a clucking, snoring sound or a long hair-raising screech.

The boobook owl's call sounds like *boo-book* or *more-pork*.
The boobook owl is also called a morepork owl.

The tawny owl
has a few different calls.
One of its calls sounds like
tu-whit-tu-who-oo-oo.

When do most owls hunt for their food?

What owls look like

Owls have large heads with eyes that look forward as they hunt for prey.

Owls' eyes are very big to let in more light. This helps them to see in the dark.

Most owls hunt for their food at night.

Owls have an extra eyelid that protects their eyes from dirt and dust.

This extra eyelid also helps keep light out of the owls' eyes during the day when they are asleep.

Why do owls have big eyes?

All sorts of owls

The **barn owl** lives on every
continent of the world
except Antarctica.

The large **snowy owl** lives
in the cold Arctic.
Its white feathers
with black marks
help it to hide
in the snow.

Owls have big eyes
to help them see in the dark.

The **boobook**
or **morepork** owl
is spotted.
When it is in danger,
it presses its feathers
close to its body,
sits up straight
and tries to look
like the tree
it is perching on.

Both the snowy
and the morepork owls
have good **camouflage**.
This means they
are hard to see.

These are only a few
of the different kinds of owls
that live around the world.

Do all owls look the same?

How owls hunt

Some birds are noisy when they fly, but owls fly silently.

They have soft, downy edges on their wing feathers.
Downy feathers do not rustle.

A mouse does not know
when an owl is swooping down.

No. There are many
different types of owls.

Owls watch and listen,
until they see or hear
something moving.

Owls' hearing is so good
that they can hear a tiny mouse
moving about in the dark.

Then they swoop down
and catch their prey in their claws.

Are owls noisy flyers or silent flyers?

How owls eat

Birds do not have teeth.
Owls pick up food in their beaks
and swallow it whole.

The food is broken up and digested
in their stomachs.

Owls are silent flyers.

After owls have finished eating, they spit out a lump or pellet. This pellet is made up of all the hard pieces of food that cannot be digested.

The pellet is made up of bone, fur, and feathers.

What is found in owl pellets?

Nests and babies

Most owls do not build nests.
They lay their eggs in a hole in a tree,
in a barn or an attic,
or in the old nest of another bird.

Bits of bone, fur, and feathers
are found in owl pellets.

The mother owl sits on her eggs to keep them warm while her chicks are growing inside.

An owl chick is called an **owlet**.

When an **owlet** is ready to hatch out of the egg, it uses a special hard tooth on the end of its beak to break the egg shell. This tooth is called an **egg tooth**. The egg tooth disappears as the owlet grows.

How does an owlet break open its shell?

Learning to fly

For the first few weeks,
the owlets wait in the nest
while their parents
hunt for food for them.

When the owlets
are a few weeks old,
they stand in the nest
and flap their wings.
This helps their muscles
to become strong
so that they
will be able to fly.

An owlet uses its egg tooth
to break open its shell.

The first time
the owlets try to fly,
they are not very good at it.

Sometimes, they make clumsy landings.

After lots of practice, the young owls become very good at flying, and can start learning to hunt for themselves.

Why do owlets stand in the nest
and flap their wings?

Where owls live

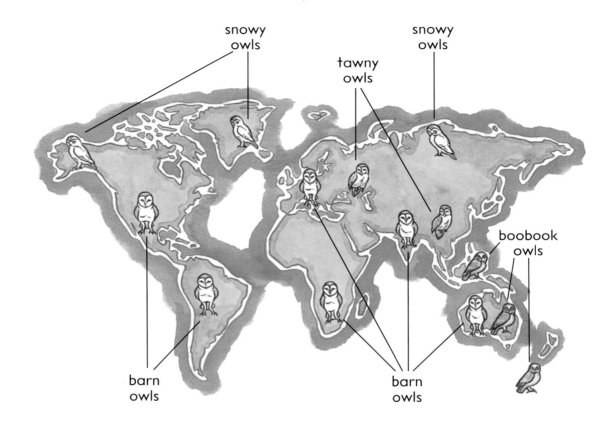

snowy owls

tawny owls

snowy owls

boobook owls

barn owls

barn owls

Owlets flap their wings to make their muscles strong for flying.